One Chance. One Vault.
One Injured Ankle . . .

The 1996 Centennial games in Atlanta found their moment of defining drama in the women's gymnastics competition. The moment that the world watched, held its breath for and will remember throughout history was provided by an eighteen-year-old American gymnast named Kerri Strug. With the team all-around gold medal hanging in the balance, she had seconds to decide whether she would be able to attempt one more vault, despite a painful injury to her left ankle from her first vault only minutes before. As she hobbled to her position, she glanced at her coaches, who shouted above the deafening cheering of the American fans who packed the Georgia Dome, "You can do it, Kerri! You can do it!" Another glance at her worried teammates—Shannon Miller, Dominique Dawes, Dominique Moceanu, Amanda Borden, Amy Chow and Jaycie Phelps—and her mind was made up.

D1508542

Books by Daniel Cohen

THE GHOSTS OF WAR
PHANTOM ANIMALS
PHONE CALL FROM A GHOST: Strange Tales from
  Modern America
REAL GHOSTS
THE WORLD'S MOST FAMOUS GHOSTS
GHOSTLY TALES OF LOVE AND REVENGE
GHOST OF THE DEEP
GUS THE BEAR, THE FLYING CAT, AND THE
  LOVESICK MOOSE: 20 Real Life Animal Stories
THE RESTLESS DEAD: Ghostly Tales from
  Around the World

Available from MINSTREL Books

GOLD MEDAL GLORY

THE STORY OF AMERICA'S 1996 WOMEN'S GYMNASTICS TEAM

DANIEL AND SUSAN COHEN

A MINSTREL® BOOK

Published by POCKET BOOKS
New York   London   Toronto   Sydney   Tokyo   Singapore

A MINSTREL PAPERBACK *Original*

A Minstrel Book published by
POCKET BOOKS, a division of Simon & Schuster Inc.
1230 Avenue of the Americas, New York, NY 10020

ISBN: 0-671-00945-1

First Minstrel Books printing December 1996

10 9 8 7 6 5 4 3 2 1

A MINSTREL BOOK and colophon are registered trademarks of
Simon & Schuster Inc.

Cover photo by Pat Hill Studio

Printed in the U.S.A.

Contents

GOLD MEDAL GLORY

CHAPTER
1

Let the Games Begin

Every Olympic games have their great moments of team competition, human drama and individual achievement. These stories are what make the Olympics the most watched event in the world every four years. More than just a sporting event, the games are truly an international phenomenon and an inspiration to millions.

The games in Atlanta, Georgia, marked the one hundredth anniversary of the Modern Olympiad, making them special and noteworthy right from the start. Many cities competed years in advance for the rights to host the games, but permission was granted to Atlanta. Olympic organizers and millions of spectators eagerly anticipated what was expected to be one of the most exciting events in history.

Thousands of reporters covered the games, and in the weeks preceding the opening ceremonies, hundreds of newspaper and magazine articles and many hours of television coverage provided profiles of many of the athletes participating in the games. For almost every sport there was some fascinating story of an individual athlete. Some overcame tremendous obstacles to compete. Some were facing the pressure of being expected to win a gold medal, and others were in Atlanta simply for the honor of representing their country and competing in a sport they loved.

The contributions of the extraordinary athletes of past Olympic games who advanced their sport and brought Olympic glory to their nations live on in our memories. Until the very last day of competition, no one could know which of the thousands of athletes, in which of the hundreds of sports, would provide the one defining moment of the Atlanta games. No one even knew if there would be that one special, magical moment that Olympic dreams are made of.

Who could forget the fantastic performance of Soviet gymnast Olga Korbut in the 1972 Munich games? Her winning personality, phenomenal talent and completely innovative moves took women's gymnastics to a new level and became an inspiration to all who followed after her. Then, in Montreal in 1976, Romanian gymnast Nadia Comaneci, inspired by Olga, surpassed her level of expertise and became the first woman in Olympic gymnastics history to ever score a perfect ten in competition. Influenced by all her predecessors, Mary Lou Retton claimed the individual all-around gold medal in the 1984 Los Angeles games. The first American woman to win the gold medal in gymnastics, Mary Lou brought a new athleticism and energy to the sport. Her influence can be seen in today's generation of powerful young gymnasts who combine grace, beauty and strength in their routines.

The 1996 Centennial games in Atlanta found their moment of defining drama in the women's gymnastics competition. The moment that the world watched, held its breath for and will remember throughout history was provided by an eighteen-year-old American gymnast named Kerri Strug. With the team all-around gold medal hanging in the balance, she had seconds to decide whether she would be able to attempt one more vault, despite a painful injury to her left ankle from her first vault only minutes before. As she hobbled to her position, she glanced at her coaches who shouted above the deafening cheer-

3

ing of the American fans who packed the Georgia Dome, "You can do it, Kerri! You can do it!" Another glance at her worried teammates, Shannon Miller, Dominique Dawes, Dominique Moceanu, Amanda Borden, Amy Chow and Jaycie Phelps, and her mind was made up.

The credo of the Olympic games is *Citius, Altius, Fortius:* "Faster, Higher, Stronger." Kerri Strug, noted *Time* magazine, may have added the word *Audacious*, "Braver," to the Olympic motto, again raising the standards of excellence in achievement for athletes and their fans to follow.

CHAPTER
2

The Vault

Shortly before the Atlanta Olympics opened, the experienced women's gymnastic team from Romania was favored by most of the experts to win the gold medal. They deserved to be the favorites. The team had won the 1994 World team championship in Dortmund, Germany, and successfully defended the title in October of 1995 in Sabae, Japan. But the Romanians also had their problems. Several of their key competitors had suffered significant injuries. Then the team had an unfortunate placement in the compulsory exercises. They were to go first. Being the first team to perform is not an advantage in gymnastics. The judges' scores usually get higher as the competition goes on. Judges are reluctant to give really high scores to the early competitors, preferring to leave room for improvement in later performances.

The Romanians did not do as well as expected and as the compulsory round ended it was clear that the real competition would be between a surprisingly strong Russian team and the American team. A highly talented but erratic Chinese team would not even make the final round.

The compulsory exercises will be eliminated in the next Olympics, but at the Atlanta games they still counted for fifty percent of the total score. As the teams moved on to the finals, the Russians had 193.796 points and the U.S. 193.669. Less than one tenth of a point separated the top two teams. It could hardly have been closer. The other two teams in the finals, the Romanians and the Ukrainians, no longer had a reasonable chance of winning the gold medal. In Olympic competition all the performances are at such a high level that a tiny point spread makes all the difference in the world. In baseball, a big inning can change the outcome of the game. In Olympic gymnastics it's almost impossible to come from far behind to win.

As the second round of competition began, it became clear that the American team, cheered on by a wildly enthusiastic hometown crowd, was going to be the team to beat.

There are four events in the women's gymnastics finals: the uneven bars, the balance beam, the floor exercise, and the vault. Six of the seven team members compete in each event. In each of the first three events, the gymnast has one chance to turn in the performance of a lifetime. In the vault, the athlete is allowed two attempts. The higher of the two scores counts toward the team total.

The Americans opened on the uneven bars and put together six clean and polished performances. Though the Russians performed well on the vault, by the time the first rotation ended, the American team had taken the lead by nearly half a point.

The Russian team turned in a magnificent effort on the uneven bars in the next exercise, but as the final rotation began, the Americans were clearly ahead. All that remained was the vault. If the team could make it through that event, they would win the gold medal. The first four Americans, Jaycie Phelps, Amy Chow, Shannon Miller, and Dominique Dawes, gave strong, clean performances, each receiving a score of 9.662 or better.

Then fourteen-year-old Dominique Moceanu, the youngest, possibly the most talented, and certainly the most highly publicized member of the team, made the first major mistake of the evening. She fell on the landing of both her Yurchenko vaults. Dominique received a high score of only 9.2. She admitted later that she had just been overwhelmed by the excitement of the Olympics.

Suddenly, assuring the American team of an Olympic gold medal was up to Kerri Strug. Kerri had never been one of the top stars of the team. Her solid talent was sometimes overshadowed by the personalities of some of her better known teammates. A strong and experienced athlete, Kerri's best event was the vault. And so she had been chosen to anchor the final event.

On her first vault the almost unthinkable happened. Kerri fell on the dismount and sprawled on the mat. Her score was a miserable 9.162. Kerri could use her second vault to get a higher score and secure the gold. But what her coaches and the breathless audience didn't know was that during the fall Kerri had felt a snap in her left ankle. When she got up she was in pain and began shaking her leg in dismay.

She later said, "I felt the gold medal was slipping away."

As she limped back up the runway she looked over at her teammates, who were urging her to shake it off. No one knew how seriously she was hurt. A temporary muscle cramp is common in gymnastics.

Up in the stands her parents were concerned. Her mother, Melanie, recalls turning to Kerri's father and saying, "Oh my gosh, something's wrong." Burt Strug tried to be optimistic and reassuring and said that it was probably only a charley horse. But even he feared it was more.

Kerri's personal coach, the legendary, flamboyant, and always controversial Bela Karolyi was leaning over the boards shouting instructions and encouragement. Kerri was in pain and asked him, "Do I have to do a second vault?"

The scores for the American and Russian teams were so close, and the scoring system so complicated, that Kerri had only minutes to make a decision. There was no time to take a break and total up the scores. The coaches and the team knew the scores were close. They just didn't know *how* close.

Karolyi said he encouraged Kerri to try the vault, but that in the end, "she was the one that had to answer that."

For Kerri the personal stakes were huge. She risked the humiliation of falling twice in a row, with the whole world watching. She risked a more serious injury. And even if things went as well as possible, it was almost certain she would seriously aggravate her ankle injury. If she were seriously injured, she would be unable to compete in the individual events or for the all-around title.

"We had no idea what the score was," said head coach Mary Lee Tracy. "What we saw was a kid who was shaking her leg but who saluted and ran down the runway."

Kerri remembers whispering a little prayer, asking "God to help me out somehow." Then she was sprinting down the runway, making her leap and landing squarely—and painfully—on both feet, holding the position just long enough for the judges to give her a score.

The score was a solid 9.712, easily high enough to erase any uncertainty about which team had won the gold. The crowd in the Georgia Dome erupted in a frenzy of cheers. They knew what the score meant.

In the meantime, Kerri had collapsed from the pain and had to be carried off the floor. Mary Lou Retton, who had won the all-around individual gold medal in women's gymnastics in 1984, had been watching from the sidelines. "She pretty much sacrificed herself," Mary Lou commented.

The medics wanted to rush Kerri to the hospital, but Karolyi—a man who, it has been said,

Kerri Strug is in pain after landing on her injured left leg following her vault routine at the summer Olympic games in Atlanta on July 23, 1996.　　(AP PHOTO/JOHN GAPS III)

never met a camera he didn't like—would have none of that! There was to be a medal ceremony photographed by hundreds of cameras from all over the world.

Kerri Strug's coach, Bela Karolyi, carries the injured athlete from the podium after she received her women's gymnastics team gold medal. (AP PHOTO/SUSAN RAGAN)

"Not even the New York City police can stop me taking you up," he said. And with that, the six-foot-plus coach swept the tiny four-foot-eight-inch gymnast up in his arms and carried her out to the medal platform for an unforgettable moment.

As the national anthem played, six tiny red, white, and blue clad gymnasts stood at attention. The seventh, Kerri Strug, stood somewhat uncertainly, but proudly, on one foot. She kept her left leg, now in a bulky cast, bent so that she didn't have to put any pressure on the swollen and painful ankle.

This moment of Olympic heroism was seen by some 32,000 spectators at the live event. But millions more watched it on television. The team gymnastics final had been taped so that it could be shown in prime time. News of the dramatic gold medal victory spread and more and more viewers tuned in, even though they knew what was going to happen.

The following day there was some discussion about whether Kerri really should have made the vault at all. In fact, even with Kerri's first low score, the American team had enough points to clinch the gold medal. But in the end her decision turned out to be fairly uncontroversial.

In recent years, women's gymnastic coaches

have been severely criticized for pushing their young charges too hard and too fast. They have been accused of risking a wide variety of serious physical and emotional injuries. But Kerri's decision was just the sort of gutsy win-one-for-the-team effort that is always praised in male athletes. Kerri Strug showed that a young woman could bring a team glory as well.

Even Joan Ryan, the author of a highly critical and influential book about women's gymnastics, said that at age eighteen Kerri was more capable of making her own decisions than a younger athlete. And with an Olympic gold medal apparently on the line she could hardly have made any other choice. "Kerri did what any of the 10,000 athletes here [at the Olympics] would have done," said Ryan.

Even though Karolyi was shouting at her, "You can do it," the choice to take a second vault was, in the end, Kerri Strug's own decision.

"I'm eighteen years old now. I can make my own choices," she said later. "I knew with Dominique falling on both vaults, the gold was slipping away. I let the adrenaline take over."

Kerri Strug's courageous and unselfish decision was one that everyone could applaud without reservation.

CHAPTER
3

The Magnificent Seven

They were called "The Magnificent Seven," though not one of them was old enough to remember where the phrase originated. It came from the title of a popular 1960 Western movie. And that movie was really a remake of a 1954 Japanese film called *The Seven Samurai.*

This Magnificent Seven didn't look like samurai warriors or cowboys, for that matter. They looked like seven tiny girls in leotards. They were the members of the U.S. women's Olympic gymnastics team. In today's world of instant sports fame and nearly instant marketing, the team's red, white, and blue jackets were already inscribed with the phrase "The Magnificent 7" long before they

The "Magnificent Seven," the 1996 United States women's gymnastics team. (AP PHOTO/JOHN GAPS III)

arrived in Atlanta. The "Mag 7" logo had already been licensed and was plastered on merchandise sold in Atlanta during the games.

Women's gymnastics is probably the single most popular sport in the modern Olympics. Oh sure, a lot of attention is paid to the basketball Dream Team, made up of famous professional players. But this team was known to be so far superior to any other team in the world that there was no suspense or excitement in any of their matches. Everyone knew who would win.

Gymnastics, on the other hand, are quick and dramatic and possess an edge-of-the-seat tension. Women's gymnastics depend more on grace than do men's gymnastics, which depend more on sheer strength. Women's gymnastics competition is a beautiful event to watch. It is a sport that seems to have been made for television.

Television is probably the most important contributor to the enormous popularity of women's gymnastics in the Olympics. Only a few hundred thousand people could afford to come to Atlanta to view the games; millions watched them on television.

The Olympics are the most widely watched television event in the world. Television networks pay huge sums of money for the rights to broadcast the games, and naturally they wish to attract the largest possible audience. Men, who tend to be generally sports minded, would probably watch the games anyway. To expand the audience, the TV networks had to broaden the appeal of the games to women viewers by emphasizing women's events and women athletes. In the summer Olympics that has meant emphasizing women's gymnastics. In the winter games it is women's figure skating that is the most watched event.

When women's gymnastics first became an Olympic sport, at the Helsinki games in 1952, it was dominated by the Eastern Europeans, particularly by women from the Soviet Union. At that time the sport was barely known in the United States. But because of the exposure it got on television its popularity grew rapidly. All over the country women's gymnastics programs were established. American girls were vaulting, tumbling, swinging, and balancing in colleges, high schools, elementary schools, community centers, and sports clubs. At first the U.S. programs were fairly primitive and it was many years before any American women had the training to really compete at a world-class level.

A major change in the fortunes of American women gymnasts came in 1981, when Bela

Karolyi, the most successful women's gymnastics coach in history, defected from his native Romania. Karolyi set up shop in the U.S. to train what he called elite gymnasts—the best of the best. These were gymnasts who could compete successfully at an international level.

By 1984 one of Karolyi's American protégées, Mary Lou Retton, took the all-around individual gold medal at the Los Angeles Olympics. True, the Soviet Union had boycotted the 1984 games, but Mary Lou's accomplishment was outstanding nonetheless. Overnight she became America's sweetheart and the popularity of women's gymnastics in the U.S. went right through the roof.

By the 1992 Olympics in Barcelona, Spain, the entire U.S. women's gymnastics team had really come of age. The team won a third place bronze medal. Individual gymnasts won silver and bronze medals in the all-around and several of the events. The Americans could successfully compete against all the finest women gymnasts in the world.

The 1992 bronze medal was the best U.S. finish to date. But unlike Mary Lou Retton's win, which was greeted with praise, these performances provoked a storm of criticism. From the time he arrived in the U.S., Karolyi's training methods had been controversial. He emphasized younger and smaller athletes. The 1976 women's team averaged five foot, three and a half inches, 106 pounds, and seventeen years. The typical 1992 team member stood four foot nine, weighed 83 pounds, and was sixteen. Karolyi's stars were sometimes as young as thirteen or fourteen. There were complaints that his Eastern European-style training methods were too rigorous and harsh. Some felt that coaches like Karolyi were endangering the physical and emotional health of their young charges. Karolyi shot back that the old-style U.S. coaches were just jealous of his successes.

While the 1992 team came back with an unprecedented number of medals for the United States, they had left a very bad impression. The team members were all so small and so young and they seemed to go through their paces mechanically, without smiling. They were dubbed "kindergarten robots."

"The media and the public were horrified at the sight of these unhappy, emaciated little girls," said critic Joan Ryan. "You could see the pain on their faces every time they performed a skill."

Kerri Strug, who, at age fourteen, was the youngest member of that team, agreed that they were a pretty unhappy bunch. "I looked at the

Coach Mary Lee Tracy, co-head coach of the 1996 U.S. women's gymnastics team, with Jaycie Phelps and Amanda Borden. (AP PHOTO/WADE PAYNE)

other national teams, and they treated each other like sisters, but we were competing like crazy to beat each other at the nationals and trials, and then, with two weeks before the games, they told us to act like a team. We were miserable.''

Stung by all the criticism, an angry and hurt Bela Karolyi announced that he was resigning from coaching women's gymnastics forever. He blamed the over-commercialization of the sport for putting too much pressure on the gymnasts.

As it turned out Karolyi's "permanent" retirement lasted only two years. When he came back he was no longer coach of the U.S. women's Olympic team, but his influence was still very strongly felt.

His wife, Marta, and Mary Lee Tracy of Cincinnati were now the two team coaches. But Bela Karolyi was there as personal coach to Moceanu

Coach Marta Karolyi, co–head coach of the 1996 U.S. women's gymnastics team, congratulates Kerri Strug. Husband Bela Karolyi looks on.

(AP PHOTO/SMILEY N. POOL, *HOUSTON CHRONICLE*)

and Strug, and he remained an obvious and even dominating presence throughout the games.

Some observers of gymnastics thought that two years away from competition had softened and improved Karolyi. He was no longer such a hard-driving task master; he was friendlier and more supportive. He always seemed to be hugging one of his charges. But in the gym Karolyi remained a tough and demanding coach with a fierce desire to win.

Criticism of coaching techniques has had an effect on women's Olympic gymnastics in general. At the Olympic games in Sydney, Australia, in the year 2000, the minimum age for the team will be raised from fifteen to sixteen. USA Gymnastics, the sport's governing body, has become increasingly aggressive in monitoring elite gymnasts and their coaches. All the gymnasts and their coaches must attend USA Gymnastics meetings with a national-team sports psychologist and nutritionist and be safety certified. Kathy Scanlan, the organization's president says that few, if any, other Olympic sports require such rigorous certification.

Certainly no one was going to call the Mag 7 kindergarten robots. With the exception of Dominique Moceanu, who just met the age requirement, turning fifteen in September, the girls were older, larger, and more experienced. Five of the seven team members were eighteen or over. In past years, conventional wisdom would have deemed them too old to compete. These athletes also specialized in the artistry and ballet of their sport rather than just the muscular acrobatics of the past.

"Technically, women's gymnastics has gone just about as far as it can," Kerri Strug says. "There's a limit to what you can do, no matter how small you are. I think judges and audiences will respond to the artistry that more mature girls bring to the sport."

U.S. women's gymnastics is now rich in talent. In 1996 there were probably more than a dozen girls good enough to make the Olympic team. Of the fourteen competitors who came to the Olympic trials in Boston, nine already had world championship experience. And that did not count Shannon Miller and Dominique Moceanu, who didn't have to compete in Boston to qualify. Both were nursing injuries. Miller, who in early June won the nationals in Knoxville, had tendinitis in her left wrist. Moceanu had a stress fracture in her right tibia. Their injuries did not hamper their performances in Atlanta and each had virtually been assured a place on the Olympic team because of her past performances. If they had been required to compete at Boston they probably would have qualified anyway.

Even those who missed making the team accepted the results with remarkable calm. Mary Beth Arnold, who finished seventh at the trials, was competing with a stress fracture similar to Moceanu's. "I knew only five places were open," said Theresa Kulikowski, who finished sixth, missing the team by one spot. "If those two were in the meet they'd have finished on top anyway." The feeling was that Miller and Moceanu really did merit special treatment because of past performances.

The team that emerged from the Olympic trials seemed to truly appreciate the value of teamwork. They were ready to work together to win the gold. They felt that they had something to prove as an American *team* performing in front of an American audience. The American women's gymnastics team was certainly not a pre-Olympic favorite to win the gold. However, with the home court advantage, they were generally regarded among the top contenders.

The American team was obviously a happier group than the 1992 team had been. They smiled and joked among themselves. Clearly they were having a great time, despite the enormous pressures of Olympic competition.

But the pressures were real enough. The U.S. squad worked with single-minded determination in pursuit of the team gold medal. In Atlanta, instead of staying in luxury hotel suites like members of the basketball Dream Team or in the Olympic Village like most of the other athletes, they lived in a fraternity house at Emory University. The team was attended by a small army of coaching technicians, sports psychologists, nutritionists, and by its own chef. On noncompetition days, the girls worked out from 8:30 in the morning until 8:30 at night, returning to the fraternity house for a lunch break and a chance to watch their favorite afternoon soap opera, "Days of Our Lives." Co-head coach Mary Lee Tracy said, "During the past year there's been some negative press about eating problems and everything like that. This team is the opposite of that image. There wasn't any abuse here."

Mary Lee Tracy, Marta Karolyi, and the five personal coaches for the different team members constantly emphasized the ideal of making the team come first. "We all sat in the room together trying to do what was best for the U.S.A." said Tracy.

There was also a recognition that there was

something in life beyond gymnastics. Coach Lori Forster told a writer for the magazine *Harper's Bazaar:* "Of course, we'd love to see these girls win gold medals, but we also want them to be happy and successful in life. As coaches, we have a responsibility in shaping these girls' lives. We don't know if a system that produces well-adjusted kids can also produce champions. But if it doesn't and if the girls come out of here feeling good about what they've accomplished, then we've done our job."

If the press was looking for more kindergarten robots, they weren't going to find them on this team. That's why there was almost no backlash regarding the injured Kerri Strug's second vault. No one felt she was a robot, a poor little girl who was pushed beyond her limits. She was a seasoned athlete doing her best for the team. That perception made all the difference in the world.

It was probably inevitable that after the emotional high of winning the team gold, there would be a letdown in the remaining events. As expected, Kerri's injury kept her out of further competition. In fact she was hobbling around on crutches. Several of the other team members were given a good chance to win the all-around title. But despite strong starts they faltered badly and were out of the running. The all-around gold medal went to Ukranian gymnast Lilya Podkopayeva—not an entirely unexpected win since she also happened to be the defending World's champion.

There were moments of tears and bitter disappointment for the Americans in the later competition. Still, in the end, nothing could diminish the glory of the team victory. The seven were truly magnificent in Atlanta.

KERRI STRUG

Kerri Strug was an unlikely heroine.

A member of the 1992 Olympic team and a seasoned veteran of international competition, she had never experienced the visibility of some of her better known teammates.

Not anymore.

Before "the vault" it had been possible for her to walk down the street unrecognized. Since July 23, 1996, she can't go anywhere without drawing an admiring crowd. For a short time she tried a disguise: a hat with an attached ponytail. Kerri normally wears her hair quite short, but the disguise didn't work. "People still recognized me."

Merely four feet nine inches, and weighing only 78 pounds, Kerri Strug was the second smallest member of the team. Only fourteen-year-old Dominique Moceanu was smaller. Kerri also has a high-pitched voice and a slightly tentative way of speaking. All of this makes her look and sound a lot younger than she really is. At eighteen years of age Kerri Strug is an experienced athlete with years of training and international competition behind her.

Kerri comes by her small stature naturally. "She comes from a little family," said one of her former coaches, Tom Forster. "Her father is under five-six and her mother is under five feet."

Kerri Strug was born on November 19, 1977, in Tucson, Arizona, where her father, Burt, is a cardiovascular surgeon. Gymnastics was a Strug family tradition. Both her older sister and brother have competed in the sport, but it was Kerri who became the international competitor.

In contrast to the stereotype of young athletes who are pushed relentlessly by ambitious parents, Kerri wasn't pushed at all. It was her own decision to try to become an Olympic gymnast, and it was a decision her parents didn't always agree with. When at age twelve she announced that she wanted to leave home in Tucson to continue her training elsewhere her mother objected strongly. "I was devastated," said Melanie Strug. "It was really hard because my son was leaving for college." But if you're going to compete in world class gymnastics you have to make hard decisions like that. Her parents always supported Kerri's decisions.

Like all elite gymnasts she started early, in 1982, when she was only five. In 1991 she made the big move, leaving her Tucson home for Houston, Texas, to train with the famous Bela Karolyi.

Karolyi knew how to produce champions. But his hard-driving style was also well known. To commit herself to this sort of life could not have been an easy decision for a thirteen-year-old.

Kerri's commitment to the sport was immediately obvious and her talents and strengths were quickly noticed in the gymnastics world. The same year she joined up with Karolyi she took a silver medal in the World Championships.

A year later, at the age of fourteen, she became the youngest Olympian representing America at the 1992 games in Barcelona. And, of course, she collected a bronze medal along with the other members of the women's gymnastics team.

After that there was a whole string of less well known but still vitally important wins and honors. Kerri has been a member of five world championship teams since 1991. In 1993 she was a world championship event finalist. In 1994 she won a silver team medal in the World Championships. She was a bronze medalist in the World Championships in 1995. Kerri won the McDonald's American Cup in 1996 and she had been a senior member of the national team since 1991. She was also the 1995 Olympic Festival Champion. Kerri's experience in such meets helped prepare her for the intense pressures of the Olympics.

Kerri Strug is well known and well respected in the world of elite women gymnasts. But to the general public, those who have only a casual interest in the sport, she was barely known at all. She had always performed in the shadow of others. First it was Kim Zmeskal and Betty Okino, her training partners at the Karolyi gym in Houston, that grabbed the media spotlight. Then came the impressive Dominique Dawes, and finally America's darling, the talented and colorful fourteen-year-old, Dominique Moceanu.

But on July 23, 1996, in the Georgia Dome, Kerri Strug stepped out of the shadows forever. And her life will never be the same again.

There has never been any doubt about Kerri's desire to excel in her chosen sport. Anyone who has seen her pacing up and down before she is ready to compete in an event can sense her determination. During training she always pushes herself to do more. Indeed some coaches think that she is too intense for her own good. She often had trouble sleeping and could be tense and high strung. "Always we were trying to get her to slow down," said Geza Pozsar, the gymnastic choreographer who came from Romania with the Karolyis' back in 1981. "We would be saying 'Kerri, just focus.'"

In 1992, when Bela Karolyi temporarily retired

from coaching, Kerri Strug had to find a new coach. First she went to Brown's Gymnasium in Orlando, Florida. But after her coaches, Rita and Kevin Brown, divorced, Kerri moved on to Dynamo Gymnastics in Oklahoma City to work with the highly successful and enthusiastic Steve Nunno. She wasn't happy at Dynamo and in 1994 Kerri returned home to Tucson to finish her senior year of high school.

Unfortunately, the coaching situation at home was far from ideal. Jim Gault, the University of Arizona coach who had worked with Kerri as a child, could not help her because of recruiting restrictions imposed by the National Collegiate Athletic Association. So after graduation, Kerri went to Colorado Springs to train at the Aerials Gymnastics Club run by Tom and Lori Forster. The Forsters had the reputation of being among the most easygoing gymnastics coaches around. However, a relaxed atmosphere was not what Kerri Strug was looking for.

Tom Forster was always realistic about Kerri's future with his club. "I knew from the beginning she wasn't intent on finishing out her career with us. She never said that, but you don't move five times and then decide on a club like ours that has never produced an Olympian."

Forster was right. When Bela Karolyi decided to

end his retirement and come back to coaching, Kerri was quick to join up with him again. She returned to her old training center in Houston. Bela and Marta Karolyi had prepared her for her first Olympic games and Kerri's goal was to compete in the 1996 Olympics. The competition would be strong and she was going to need all the help she could get to make the team again.

Kerri is very loyal to Karolyi, saying, "He is a tough coach. If he wasn't so successful he wouldn't get criticism. It's not right how everyone tries to find fault."

She believes her decision to return to the Karolyis was correct. "Everyone has their niche, and I think I've been enough places to know mine. There is no questioning Bela's and Marta's record for producing Olympic medalists."

Kerri was right. In March of 1996 she won her first major international championship, the McDonald's American Cup, in Fort Worth, Texas. In an important come-from-behind victory, Kerri was able to beat Uzbekistan's Oksana Chousovitina, who had been leading in the competition till the very end.

"I think pride made her finally come out of her shell this year," said Bela Karolyi. "And since the American Cup, where she tasted the satisfaction of individual performance, she was like a totally new person. Suddenly she was prepared to be a star."

Before 1996, critics claimed that Kerri's routines were inconsistent. In high-level competition this is a serious flaw. She also had a reputation as a worrier. She worried most about injuries— even minor ones. According to one coach, "The littlest hurt and she'd make the biggest production of it." Even Karolyi has said that she was never "one of my roughest and toughest kids."

When the lineups for the Atlanta Olympic competition were announced by the U.S. coaches, Kerri was surprised to find herself in a key and pressure-packed role. She was picked to lead off the competition on the uneven bars, usually her worst event. She would also go first on the balance beam and she would anchor the team on the floor exercises and the vault. She knew the coaches were trying to take advantage of her experience in the 1992 Olympics, "But I don't think anyone should have that much pressure on them." True to her reputation, Kerri was worried.

Then, in one spectacular instant, Kerri earned a totally new reputation as a true Olympic champion. But even after winning the gold medal Kerri was still worrying a bit. "I've had a lot of mixed

Kerri Strug grimacing in pain following her heroic second vault at the Atlanta games. (AP PHOTO/SUSAN RAGAN)

emotions," she said. "It's great that the U.S.A. won the gold medal and made history. I'm ecstatic about that. But I'm upset about my injury."

In addition to being known as a hard-driving worrier, Kerri was also described as a sensitive teammate, the one most attuned to the feelings of the other girls. Kerri was the one who remembered birthdays and sent cards and notes. She was always thought of as a team player, not the sort of athlete who tries to deliberately put down others.

Kerri is determined to excel in everything she does, not just gymnastics. She's a straight-A student who graduated from high school a year early. And she's organized. Her mother says, "You open Kerri's closet and all the short-sleeved shirts are with the short-sleeved shirts, and the long-sleeved shirts with the long-sleeved shirts. Her room is always neat. The bed is always made."

Kerri has many of the same personal traits as her heart surgeon father. "My drive comes from being a perfectionist. I got that from my dad. We put everything into whatever we do." Surgery and gymnastics are very different, but both require extensive training, skill, and attention to detail. In either pursuit the smallest slip can have disastrous results.

Kerri had always been modest about her talent.

Unlike some of her better known teammates, she didn't have an agent or any big-money endorsements. In fact she avoided high-paying endorsements, which would have taken away her amateur status, because she planned to attend UCLA after the Olympics. She wanted to study communications and continue to compete in gymnastics at amateur intercollegiate meets.

But now everything has changed. Kerri Strug is famous. She's a major celebrity. She visited the White House and met the President. There have been endless interviews and appearances. She was featured on a half-dozen national magazine covers. Within the first few weeks after Atlanta she was on "The Rosie O'Donnell Show" and "The Tonight Show With Jay Leno." She's acted in an episode of "Beverly Hills 90210" (her favorite TV show). In today's world of big-money celebrity athletics Kerri Strug now stands to earn millions. "It's exciting and at the same time scary for me," she says, "because I don't have complete control. For the first time in my life I don't know where I'm going. It's weird."

Before Atlanta, daily life was very predictable. She was up in the morning at 7 A.M. to train until 11. Then there was a rest period, lunch, and more training from 4 P.M. to 7:30.

"Every day was the same, over and over. I knew

it would take that to be good. Now every day is different. I meet exciting people. Before, I was isolated. It's a lot more fun now."

Her change from gymnast to famous person has been dramatic. "I went from wearing all leotards to wearing DKNY evening dresses and high heels—I've never worn high heels except once," she told *Washington Post* reporter Sharon Waxman. "I'd never flown first class before. The seats are a lot bigger and the stewardesses are a lot nicer. When I found out I was going to the president's birthday party, I said to my mom, 'I never even went to my friends' birthday parties. Now I'm going to the president's.'"

In the weeks after Atlanta she was in an almost perpetual state of surprise. "I keep thinking—how did this happen? How did all this come about? It seems like I just did my job; I think any athlete would have done what I did." Actually she is still disappointed that her injury kept her from competing for an individual medal. "Ever since I was little, my dream was to become an Olympic champion. I had high expectations to win an individual medal."

Still, fame has helped ease her disappointment. Kerri, who never dreamed she might be on a television show, now doesn't rule out acting as a possible career. "It'd be nice. I've never had acting lessons, or been on this side of the world," she says.

Her new agent, Leigh Steinberg, is more practical. "She's not a threat to Meryl Streep at this point," he observes. "The first stage is keeping her profile high. Keeping her name recognition high."

Kerri's parents insist on one thing: school comes first. "That's not negotiable," says Burt Strug. Her two siblings already have professional degrees. But Kerri's college career has been put on temporary hold while she enjoys the rewards of her Olympic fame.

Kerri knows that this sort of celebrity status can fade. "I don't know if I want to be in this industry," she says of the world of show business and endorsements. "These last weeks have been so exciting. This is great . . . but there's no guarantee it will last forever." And she adds, "I'm still the same Kerri I was a few weeks ago."

One thing is clear. Kerri Strug has earned her place in Olympic history. Her courageous vault will be part of every Olympic highlight show and her name will come up every time dramatic Olympic moments are recalled.

SHANNON MILLER

Shannon Miller was the most experienced of the Magnificent Seven. In many ways she probably typified the team and the new look of U.S. women's gymnastics better than any other single athlete.

Shannon had been one of the "pixies," the kindergarten robots at the 1992 games. Only fifteen years old when she went to Barcelona, she stood four foot seven and weighed 70 pounds. By 1996 she had shot up five inches. She refused to tell reporters what her weight was, but she was muscular and mature and clearly weighed more than 70 pounds.

Before the games she insisted, "We're going to have a very different team this time. We're going to be bigger, stronger, and more mature. There are things the younger, smaller girls do well, but there are advantages to being older, such as experience, strength, and artistry."

There certainly have been advantages for Shannon. Early in 1996 she won her second national title at the Coca-Cola National Championships. Overall she is the most decorated American gymnast in history, male or female. She has earned seven Olympic medals and nine World Championship medals. She is the only American in history to win two consecutive World Championships all-around titles. At the Atlanta games Shannon added an individual gold medal in the balance beam to her team gold.

In the months leading up to the Atlanta games there had been speculation that Shannon, at age nineteen, might not make the team. Some thought she was too old. As one reporter put it, she is over 100 "in gymnastics years."

Her coach, the ever-optimistic Steve Nunno, dismissed such suggestions as nonsense. "People are saying this is kind of crazy, she's over the hill, she'll never make it. If we listened to everybody else, we'd have been through a long time ago, but Shannon's actually gotten better since the [1992] Olympics. She's the Martina Navratilova of gymnastics. She has kept loving the sport, so why get out?"

"Two generations [of gymnasts] have come and gone and still Shannon is competing and setting the standard," said Nunno before the Atlanta games. In a sport where burnouts are common, Shannon Miller's long career is remarkable.

One of Shannon's problems has always been that sometimes she doesn't look as if she loves the

Shannon Miller in her gold medal performance on the balance beam at the 1996 summer Olympic games in Atlanta.

(AP PHOTO/ELISE AMENDOLA)

sport. During her routines she is tremendously focused and rarely flashes a smile. Her coaches say that they have encouraged her to become more involved with her routines, to show more feeling, to better connect with the audience and the judges, to smile more. But that's not really Shannon's style. "I'm not a bubbly person," she admits. Her best event is the balance beam, the most treacherous of all the events. "It's more important for me to stay focused than to reach the audience. You have to stay focused to stay on a four-inch beam."

Shannon Miller is not only focused, she's tough. She has a reputation for performing despite injury and pain. She is in control of every moment of a routine.

Gymnastics is a physically demanding sport. In match after match the athlete's body takes a tremendous pounding; injuries are inevitable. Over the years Shannon has had her share and then some. She was suffering from acute tendinitis in her left wrist before Atlanta and wasn't able to take part in the trials. Because of her great reputation she was guaranteed a spot on the team anyway.

Emergency surgery to put a steel pin in Shannon's dislocated elbow could have ended her chances for the 1992 Olympics in Barcelona. Instead, Shannon missed only one day of training and took the silver medal in the all-around competition.

In 1994, Shannon won her second world title while competing with a painful injured hamstring. Indeed, her willingness to play with pain is legendary and controversial. Nunno's assistant, Peggy Liddick, bristles at the criticism. "It's nothing but sexism. When Shannon Miller competed with a hamstring injury, her coaches were the meanest people on earth. When [a college football player] plays with an injured hamstring, he's gutsy and no one calls his coach abusive."

Shannon Lee Miller was born on March 10, 1977, in Rolla, Missouri, the middle child of Ron and Claudia Miller. Six months after she was born the family moved to Edmond, Oklahoma. Her father was a physics professor at the University of Central Oklahoma, and her mother was vice president of a local bank.

Shannon became interested in gymnastics at about age five, when her parents bought a trampoline. Pretty soon she and her sister were flipping and tumbling, not only on the trampoline, but in the house as well. Fearing their daughters were "going to kill themselves," as Shannon put it, her parents enrolled the two girls in gymnastics classes at a local club. "My sister stayed a couple of years and left for other things, but I loved it."

Shannon made tremendous progress and soon she was on a junior elite team aspiring to compete internationally. As part of the program, in the summer of 1986 she, together with her mother, spent two weeks at a gymnastics training camp in what was then the Soviet Union. At the time it was the world's center for women's gymnastics.

The experience was a turning point for Shannon. She realized that gymnastics was not only an activity she enjoyed, but a sport she wanted to master. "I realized [then] that it takes a lot of hard work. We worked out there a lot harder than we did at home, and I saw how good the Soviets were, and I realized I wanted to be that good."

Not only did Shannon see what the Russians were doing, the Russians saw what Shannon could do and they were impressed as well. Her father recalled, "Russians came and talked to my wife and said, 'This girl, she needs gymnastics, high-level gymnastics.'" That's when she switched from training at a local club to Steve Nunno's Dynamo Gymnastics. Nunno, a former gymnast himself, had worked briefly with Bela Karolyi and had some of the Romanian wizard's hard-driving style. He appreciated Shannon's determination. "Shannon is the hardest worker in my gym, and always has been."

It was Nunno's philosophy to try to have Shannon always perform above her ability. "I made sure that she was doing the big skills from day one, skills that were way beyond what she thought she could do. But she was willing to try them, so I was willing to go with it."

In her early matches Shannon wasn't a standout and she fell a lot. But she kept on plugging and kept on moving up. By the 1992 Olympic trials she had piled up an impressive number of wins. But she remained relatively unknown compared with Karolyi's well-publicized gymnasts. However, in the trials Shannon actually finished ahead of the favored Kim Zmeskal. Shannon's win caused a famous outburst of bad temper from Zmeskal's coach, Bela Karolyi. He simply refused to acknowledge that Shannon had won the trials.

Shannon justified her ranking in the trials by her performance at the Barcelona games. She won a silver in the all-around, missing the gold by only .012 points. She was the first American gymnast to win five Olympic medals since Mary Lou Retton in the 1984 games.

After the Barcelona games Shannon was a star. There were tours, talk shows, lucrative endorsements, and the novelty of being recognized by strangers on the street. This was great on the one hand, but for a basically shy person it was also difficult. Shannon tried hard to live a normal life. "I still go to public school," she told a writer for *Sports Illustrated* in December 1992. "I still work out, my coach still yells at me in the gym. My brother and sister still pick on me, and I still pick on them. Many of my friends have known me since I was in first grade, and they treat me the same."

After her spectacular performance in the 1992 Olympics, Shannon continued to pile up wins. But she also piled up injuries. By mid 1994 she was suffering from a pulled stomach muscle and shin splints. She still managed to win gold in the all-around and a second gold on the beam in the World Gymnastics Championships in Brisbane, Australia. "This means even more to me because I had to come back from injuries," she said.

Later that year Shannon lost her national championship to Dominique Dawes. Then she finished poorly at the 1995 American Cup. She came in second at the 1995 nationals, and then lost her world title. Many observers began to speculate that she was over the hill.

"I don't mind getting called old, because I'm only eighteen," she said, "but I don't think it's going to affect me. I've been able to learn some new skills and I plan to keep learning until '96."

Coach Nunno also expressed confidence. "They'll need her experience and leadership at the Olympics."

He was absolutely right. Kerri Strug's brave vault was the dramatic high point of the team gold medal performance. But it was Shannon's solid performance in all the events that put the U.S. team in the lead in the first place.

Shannon lists her hobbies as swimming, shopping, and watching TV—all very normal for a teenaged American girl. She also collects sports pins, a hobby many other Olympic athletes share. At every international sporting event there are all sorts of little enameled pins available. They can be team pins, game pins, pins from the city in which the event is held, or pins from other countries. The athletes often trade these pins with one another. Shannon began trading pins on her first trip to the gymnastics camp in the Soviet Union in 1986 and has been at it ever since. Now she has hundreds of pins from all over the world. "As I get older, I will be able to look at a pin and remember the competition at which I got it. It's kind of neat," she says.

One story about Shannon shows the kind of person she is. When she graduated from Edmond North High School in May 1995, she had a near perfect 3.96 grade point average. The only thing that kept her from a perfect academic score was that she could never get higher than a B in geometry as a sophomore. Darrell Allen, the math teacher who gave her that less than perfect grade, became ill with leukemia in 1994. His family faced staggering medical bills. So Shannon organized a celebrity auction with donations from fellow Olympians like Bonnie Blair, Dan Jansen, and Greg Louganis. The auction raised more than $5,000 for Allen, who died seven days later. Like many Olympians Shannon has done a lot of charity work, but this was certainly one of her most personal efforts.

What does the future hold for Shannon Miller? She has already stayed at the top of a sport geared to very young women longer than practically anyone believed she could.

Shannon had planned to retire from gymnastics after the 1996 games. She had already taken courses at the University of Oklahoma during the 1995–96 academic year and plans to continue her education there. She has talked about going into the field of sports medicine. But because of the fame and fortune that have followed the American gymnastics team's gold medal victory, all her plans are on hold, at least for a while. And why not? Shannon may be the senior citizen of the U.S. women's Olympic gymnastics team. But she won't even turn twenty until March 1997. She has plenty of time to plan her future.

DOMINIQUE MOCEANU

Dominique Moceanu is not only a world class gymnast, she is also a best-selling author—and she's only fifteen!

Dominique was born to be a gymnast. When Dominique's father, Dimitry, first saw his newborn seven-pound-six-ounce infant daughter he told his wife, Camelia, "She looks very strong. Looks good for a gymnast."

Like many people in their native Romania, both of Dominique's parents had been interested in the sport of gymnastics. The Romanian national team was the country's claim to world fame. But it was Dimitry Moceanu who pursued his gymnastic ambitions with unusual passion and commitment. From the age of six, he was training four hours a day.

When he was sixteen, harsh reality intruded. In Romania at that time, career choices were limited and had to be made early. Dimitry was given a choice, he could train for gymnastics full time or he could go to school full time. There was no way to mix the two. Dimitry's parents didn't think gymnastics was a practical way to make a living. They wanted their son to be a doctor. So he was forced to give up the sport he loved. But he never gave up the dream of gymnastics. He swore that his firstborn child, boy or girl, would be given the chance to become the gymnast that he had wanted to be. Dimitry called it an unfinished dream.

The way things worked out, Dimitry never became a doctor either. He finished high school. Then he had to complete three years of compulsory military service. Then he went to college for three years. However, he came to feel that there was no future for him in his native land.

The year was 1979. Romania was in the paralyzing grip of communist dictator Nicolai Ceausescu. The nation had a glittering international gymnastics team, but at home life was grim and often frightening. Romania was one of the unhappiest countries in the world. Dimitry decided that if he wanted a real future he would have to leave.

Leaving Romania wasn't easy and it wasn't safe. Passports were not issued freely because the authorities thought, correctly, that many of those who left would not come back. Dimitry applied for a passport. He received a call from government officials asking him to come down and pick it up. His family was sure this was a trap, and if he went to claim the document he would be arrested. Despite their fears Dimitry went anyway. Much to his relief, everything appeared to be in order and he was given his passport without any trouble.

He bought a ticket to Austria, telling officials at the state-run airline that he was going on a little vacation. But when the time came to return home Dimitry instead went from Austria directly to the United States, where he applied for political asylum. Such applications were routinely granted in 1979.

Dimitry went to Chicago, where he was sponsored by a church. The young refugee had no money, no relatives, and didn't know how to speak English. For the first few days he slept in the church until he found a job in a Greek restaurant called Aphrodite's. A few months later he got another job, managing another restaurant. He had begun to settle down in America. He was on his way.

Dimitry's successful move to the U.S. inspired other members of his family to try the same thing. His brother Costa came to the U.S. and went to live in California. Then Dimitry's girlfriend, Camelia, went to Greece and never returned to Romania. Dimitry went to meet her there and they were married.

After they flew back to the United States, they bought a cross-country bus ticket to Burbank,

California. Once they arrived, Costa was able to get Dimitry a job running a school cafeteria. Camelia was pregnant and trying to learn English by watching television with a Romanian-English dictionary in her hand. She learned the language quite well. Dominique was born on September 30, 1981.

Dimitry worked very hard in California and managed to save enough money to go back to Chicago and buy Aphrodite's, the restaurant where he had worked when he first came to the United States. Soon Dimitry's parents and his brother Iani came to the U.S. The family ran the restaurant—and ran it very successfully—though it took a great deal of hard work.

Almost as soon as Dominique was born, Dimitry Moceanu began looking around for ways to fulfill his own incomplete gymnastics dream. Dominique was only three and a half years old when Dimitry called his famous countryman Bela Karolyi in Houston. He wanted to bring his daughter to the Karolyi gym so that she could train for gymnastics with the best. Karolyi had often been criticized for putting very young girls into training, but even he said three and a half was too young. He told Dimitry to call back in about six years. So Dominique started her training at a local Chicago club.

The restaurant was profitable, but the family didn't like the cold Chicago winters. In 1988 Dimitry sold the business and moved his family to Florida. He opened a used car lot, Camelia worked in a beauty salon, and Dominique trained for gymnastics at a club called LaFleurs. But Dimitry's ultimate goal for his future gymnastic champion was still Houston.

There are a lot of stories in gymnastics, and other sports, about parents who pushed their unwilling children into the activity. Dimitry Moceanu was certainly anxious for his daughter to succeed in the sport that he had loved as a child, but fortunately Dominique herself had the same ambition.

When Dominique was ten years old she was watching gymnastics on television. It was obvious that all the top women gymnasts were being trained by Bela Karolyi. She said, "Oh, if only I could train with Bela." Dimitry's eyes lit up. He had never told his daughter about his first call to Karolyi. But almost immediately after her comment, he was on the phone again.

This time Karolyi was more receptive. He told Dimitry the date of his next tryouts. Over the Thanksgiving weekend, the Moceanu family drove to Houston, where Bela and Marta were testing possible pupils. Only the most promising were going to have a chance to train with the master.

The tests were grueling, but Karolyi spotted something in Dominique that he liked. "She's a fighter," he said. Dimitry Moceanu was about to see his long-delayed dream fulfilled.

Training an elite gymnast is a family affair. As soon as Dominique was accepted by Karolyi, the family, including their two-year-old daughter Christina, moved to Houston. Dimitry spent the next year and a half commuting between Houston and Tampa while he tried to sell his Florida used car lot.

As busy as he was with the traveling and his work, Dimitry often didn't have time to watch his daughter compete. Training and travel have cost the family hundreds of thousands of dollars. There hasn't been a family vacation in years. "They would do anything for me," Dominique has said.

But in the end it is the athlete herself who actually has to perform. Dominique has always shown the sort of talent and drive necessary to compete at the highest international level of gymnastics.

For Dominique stardom came quickly. In her first year with Karolyi she became the youngest

Dominique Moceanu shows the form that makes her great—
working out on the balance beam in the Georgia Dome at the
1996 summer Olympic games.   (AP PHOTO/ELISE AMENDOLA)

member ever of the U.S. junior gymnastics team. She was already being described as a cinch to make the 1996 Olympics team. She was often described as the next Nadia, a reference to Karolyi's most famous protégée, the great Nadia Comaneci.

In addition to skill and determination, Dominique had something else: personality. When she went through her routines she was able to connect with the judges and the audience. She was easy to interview and loved the attention. Unlike the serious Shannon Miller, Dominique Moceanu has a great smile, and it comes easily and naturally. She says that sometimes she has to remind herself to stop smiling and concentrate on the routine.

Nadia herself, who occasionally advised Dominique, sees similarities in their styles. She sees great differences as well. "I grew up in a different system and was taught to keep everything inside," Nadia said. "She takes all her feelings outside. That's the American way."

The wins and the honors began to pile up for the young gymnast. Dominique won the Junior National Championship when she was twelve, in 1995. At age thirteen she won the all-around event at the U.S. Senior Championships. She was the youngest Senior National Champion ever, defeating both Shannon Miller and Dominique Dawes.

The fame followed the wins. After her national championship win Dominique got some six thousand fan letters. She was featured in articles in *Time* and *People* magazines. She was photographed for the cover of *Vanity Fair* by the famous photographer Annie Liebovitz. She hired an agent to handle offers for endorsements and public appearances, and she was even featured in an Olympic television ad for Kodak. She wrote an autobiography, *Dominique Moceanu—An American Champion.* It was a short autobiography, because she was still only fourteen. With all of the Olympic excitement, the book became a bestseller.

Here is the young gymnast's daily routine as described in her book: She is up at six in the morning and has a bran muffin and fruit for breakfast. This is followed by three hours of training in the gym, a nap, and lunch, usually a grilled chicken Caesar salad. There is an hour of physical therapy, which leaves her feeling smooth and relaxed, "like a racehorse." This is followed by three or four more hours of practice, a light dinner, time for homework or watching some TV, after which she collapses into bed.

Dominique was considered an absolute shoo-in for the 1996 Olympics and a possible gold medalist in the floor exercise, her best event. Karolyi did not hold back on the publicity for his young athlete, though even he was surprised by the speed with which she progressed. At times he uncharacteristically tried to play down expectations for Dominique, perhaps fearing that she might feel too much pressure. He wanted her to "sneak up from behind in the Olympic year." But by the Olympic year she was already in front as far as the public was concerned. She wasn't going to sneak anywhere.

But gymnastics is a tough and demanding sport. The vaults, the flips, and the falls begin to take their toll. They began to have an effect on Dominique. Shortly before the Olympic trials, doctors discovered a four-inch stress fracture in her right tibia. It was the first significant injury she had received in her career. While the stress fracture was certainly not a career-threatening injury, it was a serious and a painful one. Dominique had to withdraw from the Olympic qualifying trials, and like the injured Shannon Miller, had to petition for a place on the team. Based on their past performances, it was clear that she and Miller were going to be awarded with places on the team. They deserved them. Still, this injury was both a scare, and a disappointment for Dominique. She helped the U.S. women's team win its gold medal, but she did not become the big star of the games that many of her fans had expected.

In the past it would have been assumed that her gymnastics career had already peaked in '96, but that sort of thinking doesn't really apply anymore. By the 2000 Olympics Dominique Moceanu will be only eighteen. In 1996, both Kerri Strug and Shannon Miller were participating in their second Olympics, and they did better than in their first. If Dominique stays healthy and retains her desire she can become a star of the next Olympics.

Dominique Dawes

Her friends and her coach affectionately call her Awesome Dawesome. Sometimes she seems that way—almost like a force of nature.

She is also known for taking risks. Sometimes they pay off, sometimes they don't. At the 1993 World Gymnastics Championships in Birmingham, England, it wasn't Dominique's silver medal performances on the uneven parallel bars and balance beam that got everyone's attention. It was a gamble she took in the all-around competition.

Dominique was actually leading the competition after three events with only the pommel horse vault remaining. She needed a 9.787 score to win. Her usual vault averaged 9.8, but she dropped her usual routine and tried a more difficult vault, one that she had recently been experimenting with.

The gamble didn't pay off. The experimental routine was not clean and she received a much lower than expected score. She dropped out of medal competition and wound up in fourth place.

But the performance got her noticed. "I'm really disappointed, but I'm excited that I won the silver medals," Dawes said. "I upgraded my ranking from twenty-sixth in the world to fourth in the world."

At the 1995 Coca-Cola National Championships she turned in an incredible performance, despite a stress fracture in her left wrist. Her chief competition was Shannon Miller. After Shannon stepped out of bounds in the floor exercise, all Dominique needed was a clean performance in her best event to take the gold. Instead of playing it safe, she threw in a risky back-and-forth tumbling pattern that included eleven aerial moves, and surprised even her longtime coach, Keli Hill.

Dominique Dawes was born on November 20, 1976, in Silver Spring, Maryland. That made her nineteen years old at the 1996 Olympic games. Four months older than Shannon Miller, Dominique was the oldest member of the Magnificent Seven.

She had also been a member of the 1992 women's Olympic gymnastics team. At that time she was fifteen, stood a compact four foot seven, and weighed 75 pounds. Four years later she had added thirty pounds to her weight and seven inches to her height. She had become a muscular and well-developed young woman.

Dominique really came into her own in 1994 at the National Championships when she won the all-around and four individual events. She was the

Dominique Dawes performs her bronze medal–winning floor routine at the 1996 summer Olympic games in Atlanta.

first gymnast to accomplish this feat since Joyce Tanac Schroeder won the all-around and all four events at the 1969 AAU National Championships.

Dominique Margaux Dawes first took up gymnastics at the age of six. She had a great deal of drive even when she was young. She would write the word *Determination* over and over again on a mirror in crayon, just to psyche herself up. She was also popular at Gaithersburg High School, where she was the prom queen her senior year.

Dominique is the oldest member of the American team and a natural leader. It's a role she has become accustomed to. Only the second African-American to earn a spot on the U.S. Olympic women's gymnastics team (Betty Okino made the 1992 team) and the second to win the U.S. National Championships (Diane Durham won in 1983), Dominique has been a pioneer in women's gymnastics. She is a well-known and much-loved role model for young athletes.

Dominique is instantly recognized by fans of women's gymnastics. She is also a familiar face to the general public. Her stunning routine, shown briefly in the popular Kodak Olympic commercial, grabbed viewers' attention. Of all the Magnificent Seven she is probably the most poised and personable.

Despite the trend toward older Olympic women gymnasts, Dominique does not realistically plan to make the next Olympic team at age twenty-three. Even before the Atlanta games she had enrolled at the University of Maryland. She was making plans for life beyond the world of international gymnastics competition. Of course, she'll still make time to enjoy the exhibitions, the personal appearances, and all the other opportunities that have come with being a key member of the 1996 gold medal team. Awesome Dawesome deserves them.

Jaycie Phelps

No one becomes a member of the U.S. women's Olympic gymnastics team entirely on her own. Every athlete needs a great deal of support, particularly from her family.

Jaycie Phelps's story is typical in that respect. When Jaycie was only four, her preschool class visited a gym on a field trip. The four-year-old tried a few exercises, did them well, and seemed to really be enjoying them. So although her parents, Jack and Cheryl Phelps, didn't have any previous interest in the sport, they put her into gymnastics classes. It was just something to do with an active child. They didn't have any Olympic dreams for their daughter. They had no idea where it all would lead. They certainly didn't think it was going to change their lives. But it did.

Jack and Cheryl watched in amazement as their daughter rose from one level to the next. Gymnastics start at Level 1. Competition begins at Level 4. After Level 10 gymnasts go to the elite level and work toward international competition and the Olympics.

Jaycie—the name is a combination of her parents' initials—was born on September 29, 1979, in Indianapolis, Indiana. By the time she was twelve, Jaycie's Indiana coaches told her parents that she had advanced beyond their teaching ability. If she wanted to continue to progress in the sport she would have to find new coaches.

The Phelps's found what they thought would be the right place, a gymnastics club in Arizona. The family didn't hesitate. Leaving friends and school behind, Jaycie and her older brother Dennis moved to Arizona with their parents.

The family loved Arizona, but unfortunately Jaycie's training wasn't going that well. In 1993 she finished a very disappointing twenty-fourth in the junior division of the USA Championships. Jaycie was upset and thought about giving up gymnastics completely. But her parents thought that a new gym and coach might make a lot of difference. They found the Cincinnati Gymnastics Academy. Its owner, Mary Lee Tracy, is a top coach who would later become co-head coach of the 1996 women's Olympics gymnastics team. Tracy is a coach known for her easygoing and affectionate style. The motto of the Cincinnati Gymnastics Academy is "Where Kids Go to Have Fun." Jack and Cheryl persuaded a very discouraged Jaycie to give the sport another chance.

Of course, the whole family had to move again. And this time they had to split up. Jack and

Dennis moved back to Indiana so Dennis could graduate from high school with his original class. Cheryl and Jaycie found an apartment near the gym, to make it easier for Jaycie to settle into a routine of school, then gymnastics practice.

Living apart can put a terrible strain on families. But the Phelps's were a close family and realized that this arrangement was only temporary. The arrangement worked. So did the new gym. Jaycie began winning again, and she was enjoying the sport more than she had in a long time.

One of the other students at the Cincinnati Gymnastics Academy was Amanda Borden, another possible Olympian. Since everyone knew there are only seven places on an Olympic team, the potential for a heated rivalry between the two certainly existed. But it never developed, and Jaycie and Amanda became best friends. So did their mothers. In a true happy ending, both girls made the team.

Like all gymnasts, Jaycie Phelps has had her share of injuries. Perhaps she has had more than her share. She admits, "I can't remember a day when I didn't hurt somewhere."

Jaycie's injuries have involved hairline fractures, a dislocated elbow, and countless bruises. She also has a congenital spine condition that can

Jaycie Phelps begins her routine on the uneven bars during the women's gymnastics competition at the 1996 summer Olympic games in Atlanta. (AP PHOTO/AMY SANCETTA)

give her lower back trouble if she doesn't exercise her abdominal muscles. By far her most serious injury came when the cartilage in her left knee tore during a practice session. There was no specific reason for the injury. It was just the result of the stress of repeated jumps and dismounts.

For a gymnast, a knee injury is potentially career ending. Jaycie needed surgery and five months of recuperation to recover. Still, she says that she has absolutely no regrets about the pain or the heavy work schedule. Her coach says that one of Jaycie's strongest points is her work ethic. "Her attitude is what, in competition, we call the 'ideal performance state,'" says Tracy. "She comes in relaxed, ready to have fun, ready to do anything she can do to make herself better."

Jaycie's parents worry constantly about injuries, and where to draw the line. They trust their daughter and her coach to alert them to any indications of serious trouble. They also know that playing with pain is what athletes have to do. "It's no different in gymnastics than in any sport, especially if you're a dedicated athlete," says Jack.

Like all competitive athletes, Jaycie is careful about what she eats. Before meets she sticks to meals like pasta and salad or rice and beans. She does allow herself an occasional treat, like her grandmother's homemade pies or vegetable pizza.

What does the future hold for Jaycie Phelps? At the moment she is enjoying the fame of having won an Olympic gold medal. But Jaycie is not one of the team superstars and her celebrity is likely to be short lived. She intends to go on to college and perhaps become a doctor specializing in sports medicine. Her future gymnastics activity would be limited to college meets.

She is certainly young enough and talented enough to plan for a shot at the 2000 games. Before 1996 that was only a distant possibility. Even after the Atlanta win she has no firm plans. "I really haven't thought that far," she says.

AMY CHOW

Amy Chow can play the piano almost as well as she can perform on the uneven bars. She is also a top student and plans to be a doctor. The one thing she doesn't do very well is talk. She is well known among sports reporters and interviewers for her one-word answers and long silences.

One time an interviewer became so frustrated with her one-word answers he asked if he could give her a list of written questions. She could write out the answers and give them back to him the next day. It sounded like a great plan. The problem was that when the reporter got his list back, all the written answers were either yes or no.

Amy Chow began gymnastics at the age of three. But that was only because her mother couldn't find a ballet teacher who was willing to take a three-year-old. So Susan Chow took her young daughter to the West Valley Gymnastics Club near San Jose, California. The club had just been purchased by gymnastics coach Mark Young. He was impressed. "I think she is the most exceptional kid I've ever been around," he said. Fifteen years later Young is still Amy's coach, even though others have tried to recruit the talented gymnast.

Young's associate, Diane Amos, recalls once hearing Bela Karolyi say to Amy and another one of her gymnasts, "You two look good; you two come to my gym." Incidents like this, by the way, are among the reasons that Karolyi is such a controversial figure in gymnastics.

Amy, however, showed no desire at all to join the famous coach in Houston. She wanted to remain close to her parents, she was loyal to her coach, and saw no reason to change.

"He is like a second father to me," she said. "I always kept improving, so why leave?"

Amy's real father, Nelson Chow, was born in China and at age ten went to Hong Kong, where her mother, Susan, was born. But the couple did not meet until they were both students at San Jose State, in California. Amy was born in San Jose on May 15, 1978.

Like the parents of most young gymnasts Nelson and Susan Chow have sacrificed a lot. Probably the toughest thing they faced was driving Amy from place to place. Young described how he had seen Amy's parents shuttle her—usually in the same day—from their home in San Jose to the prestigious Castilleja School in Palo Alto, then to the West Valley Club for a short training session, then back to school again, then to the gym once more before finally taking her home for the evening.

"Her mom has a bad back from being in the car so much," Young said. "I think the odometer in their car has turned over three times in the past couple of years."

Though Amy Chow has accomplished many things in her young life, learning to drive is not one of them. She has never had the time. But once the Olympic excitement dies down she expects to finally get her driver's license.

Amy has attempted some of the most difficult routines ever tried by a woman gymnast. In fact, her trademark move on the uneven bars—a backward circle around the bar to a handstand full pirouette—is named "the Chow" after her.

She has also shown great fighting spirit and drive. In the Olympic trials she had a terrible collision with the balance beam. Although she was clearly stunned by the blow to her head, she was able to regain her poise, remount the beam and finish her routine without another mistake. Her courage and determination were rewarded with a spot on the Olympic team. And her refusal to settle for anything less than her best led her to claim the silver medal on the uneven bars.

Amy Chow waves to the crowd after tying for an individual silver medal in the uneven bars competition. Next to her is Bi Wenjiing of China, who also won a silver medal.

"I enjoy doing things that people enjoy watching and not many other people can do," she said.

There is only one gymnastic skill in which she has not been able to excel: the floor exercise. It's not that she can't perform the moves as well as anyone. She can. But to get the highest scores in the floor exercise the athlete also has to smile and project her personality to the audience and the judges. This is something that Amy finds very difficult to do.

Even before the Olympics Amy had accepted a gymnastics scholarship to Stanford University. Collegiate gymnastics are nowhere near the level of competition she is used to. But the scholarship certainly will help pay for her studies. And she will always be known as an Olympic gold medal winner.

AMANDA BORDEN

In 1992 Amanda Borden came just *this* close to making the Olympic team. She was so discouraged after the near miss that she very nearly gave up on gymnastics. But she hung in there for another four years.

In 1996, at the age of nineteen, and facing stiffer competition then before, Amanda gave it another try. And at the Olympic trials she hung on and grabbed the fifth and final qualifying spot. (Two places had already been reserved for the injured Shannon Miller and Dominique Moceanu.) Amanda nailed all four of her routines and was particularly impressive on the beam, where a single misstep could have cost her an Olympic berth. Instead of missing she was nearly perfect, scoring a 9.862, the highest balance-beam mark given at the trials.

"I can't really explain what making the team means to me after just missing in '92," she said tearfully. "Dreams come true, that's what it means."

Amanda was born on May 10, 1977, in Cincinnati, Ohio. She started taking ballet lessons when she was very young. Then, when she was about seven, a teacher told her mother, Patty, that Amanda was really built more like a gymnast than a ballerina. And so Amanda's parents enrolled her in a once-a-week gymnastics class.

That was just the beginning. Amanda's talent for the sport showed quickly. The more talent she displayed, the more lessons she took. Soon she was taking gymnastics classes six days a week. The sport of gymnastics began to take over the Borden family's lives.

Luckily, Amanda was able to find a world-class coach right in her hometown. She trained with Mary Lee Tracy at the Cincinnati Gymnastics Academy. But Amanda's mother, Patty, a medical assistant, and her father, Doug, director of surgical services at a Cincinnati hospital still spent a lot of time driving Amanda around. She would go to the gym for early morning practice, then back home, then to school, then back to the gym after school, and finally home. It was a great relief to everyone when Amanda finally got her driver's license and was able to take care of her own transportation.

Amanda told interviewer Dan Gutman that gymnastics is something that "grows on you." When she started it was just for fun. She never really thought of international competition or the Olympics. She has stayed in the sport because she

Amanda Borden, high above the balance beam during the 1996 summer Olympic games in Atlanta.

(AP PHOTO/JOHN GAPS III)

enjoyed it. "I wouldn't be able to get myself out of bed at 5:30 and go into the gym every day. There are times when I don't want to go to the gym and work out, but I think any athlete experiences that. It only makes you a stronger person when you push yourself through those times."

Many elite gymnasts don't attend regular school but Amanda always has. She went to public school, then to Cincinnati's Finneytown High School, graduating in June of 1995. She was a top student and 1994 homecoming queen.

Amanda is a naturally outgoing person. She smiles a lot and looks as if she is having fun performing. Even when things are not going well she is able to smile. In fact, her nickname is "Pepsodent."

Amanda has another good trait for a gymnast. It's easy for her to resist junk food. Unlike some other gymnasts who have to struggle and sacrifice to stay small, Amanda is not a big eater. While some gymnasts dream about candy bars while dieting, Amanda does not crave sweets. She says that she could do without them entirely if she had to. In fact, she says her favorite food is tuna.

Amanda's decision to stay with gymnastics after missing a spot on the 1992 Olympic team eventually paid off. After her 1992 disappointment and decision to stay with gymnastics she won a silver medal in the team competition at the World Championships in 1994. At the 1995 Pan-American Games she won on the balance beam and floor exercise and took third in the all-around. And then, of course, she made the Olympic team in 1996.

Before the Olympics she had already received an athletic scholarship to the University of Georgia. She plans to follow in her parents' footsteps and be a part of the medical profession, but with a sports angle. She is thinking about working with other athletes as a physical therapist, nutritionist, or sports psychologist.

CHAPTER
4

Bela Karolyi

You have certainly noticed that the name Bela Karolyi has come up regularly in the previous chapters. It's impossible to talk about women's gymnastics today without talking about Karolyi. There is no doubt he has changed women's gymnastics more than any other single coach.

Karolyi was born in a mountainous part of Romania called Transylvania. In America everyone knows Transylvania as the home of the legendary vampire, Count Dracula. Karolyi swears that he never even heard of Dracula or vampires until he came to America.

Karolyi's home was a small coal mining town in the poorest part of Romania. Bela was a large,

Coach Bela Karolyi reacts with joy as his student Kerri Strug finishes a nice routine on the balance beam during the 1996 U.S. Olympic trials in gymnastics on Sunday, June 30, in Boston. (AP PHOTO/ELISE AMENDOLA)

strong boy who excelled in some of the rougher sports like rugby. He got into a college program that trained coaches and physical education teachers. At the time he had no particular interest in gymnastics. But another student, Marta Eross introduced him to the sport.

Marta and Bela were married on November 28, 1963. They had jobs teaching physical education in two small towns near where Bela was born. They were good teachers and the programs were extremely successful.

At that time Romania didn't really have a strong gymnastics tradition. The country had only won two Olympic bronze medals in its history. But the Romanian communist government, like many other Eastern European communist governments, saw sports as a way of gaining international recognition and prestige. So while most of the country was desperately poor and neglected, the government began pouring money into developing an elite, world class sports program. Bela Karolyi was chosen to set up the national school of gymnastics. He didn't really have an international reputation as a coach. He was just the best the Romanians had at the time. And he was a whole lot better than anyone expected.

As Karolyi tells the story, he set out on a bicycle trip around the country going from school to school trying to find promising young gymnasts. In 1968 in the town of Oneşti, he saw two little girls in the school yard turning cartwheels and doing handstands. He was impressed. But just as he was about to go over to them, the school bell rang and the children rushed inside. Karolyi followed them, running from classroom to classroom until he found them.

As you can probably already guess, one of the girls was to become the most famous gymnast in the world, Nadia Comaneci. The other was Viorica Dumitro, who was to become one of Romania's best ballerinas.

In a poor country like Romania there were definite advantages in being chosen for one of the sports programs. The athletes received free food, lodging, and education. And if they were successful, they became national heroes.

The down side was that children as young as six could be whisked away from their families and friends. Training methods were harsh and would have been unacceptable in the United States.

Karolyi was a tough gymnastics coach. He treated his young charges as if they were professional football players. They worked out for hours every day, often seven days a week. He would scream at them and humiliate them if they made mistakes. There was no one making sure that they were eating correctly or preventing them from competing while they were injured. Many young

Romanian girls simply broke down under the treatment. Those who didn't became some of the best gymnasts in the world.

Karolyi's Romanian team burst upon the world scene at the 1976 Montreal Olympics. When the team first marched out they were described as looking like a "bunch of elves." The entire group was outfitted with white leotards with red piping and had pigtails held in place by red and white bows. They were all about Nadia's size, four feet eleven inches and 85 pounds.

The Russian team, led by Olga Korbut, was expected to dominate the competition. But then Nadia and the other Romanians began doing tricks that no woman gymnast had ever accomplished before. The crowd and the judges were simply awed. Few remember that the Russians actually won the team competition. Strong performances by Olga and her teammates were overshadowed by Nadia's perfect 10 scores—the first in women's Olympic gymnastics. Nadia also won several individual events. It was her image that dominated the games. And right there with the tiny, quiet gymnast was her coach, the huge and very loud Bela Karolyi. He became nearly as famous as Nadia herself.

However, Karolyi's fame and his tendency to speak his mind whenever he felt like it began to get him in trouble back at home. Romania's leader, Nicolae Ceausescu, was deeply suspicious of anyone who showed any independence. Soon, the funds to Karolyi's gym were cut and some of his best pupils, including Nadia, were taken away from him. The Romanian authorities suspected that he was planning to defect and were watching him closely.

In his autobiography Karolyi insists that he had not thought of defecting up to that point. But the government was beginning to make life so hard for him that he felt he had no choice.

In 1981 Karolyi led the Romanian gymnastics team on an American exhibition tour. The tour would make a lot of money for the Romanian Gymnastics Federation. Karolyi accepted the assignment reluctantly. When the time came for the team to fly back to Romania from New York, Bela and Marta Karolyi and choreographer Geza Pozsar slipped out of their hotel and went to Marta's aunt's apartment. They happened to choose the day on which President Ronald Reagan was shot. When Bela, who spoke no English, first saw the scene on television he said, "To me it looked like any other gangster movie." Then, when he found out what had happened, he began to wonder what he had gotten himself into.

Even with the attempted assassination of a

president, Karolyi's defection made big news. After a few months of real hardship, Karolyi was able to get enough financial backing to establish a training center for elite gymnasts in Houston, Texas.

Karolyi's career as a coach in the United States has been stormy. In Romania, at least until he began getting into trouble with the government, he was the absolute ruler of women's gymnastics. He set the training schedule, he picked the team. No one questioned him because his teams won. In the U.S., things were done differently. There were lots of other coaches he had to contend with. His battles with other gymnastics coaches became legendary.

Karolyi's strict and rigorous training techniques did not fit comfortably with America's ideas of what sports should be about, especially for young girls. There was criticism that the routines he had his girls do were too dangerous. The famous professional football coach Vince Lombardi claimed that "winning is the only thing," but clearly that philosophy did not apply to twelve-year-old girls.

Karolyi certainly produced American champions like Mary Lou Retton. He helped to make America a genuine women's gymnastics international powerhouse. But he was widely criticized, and that is what led to his brief retirement after the 1992 Olympics.

Some feel we are now seeing a kinder and gentler Bela Karolyi. He has certainly earned the loyalty and gratitude of many of his athletes, like Kerri Strug.

One thing is certain: Bela Karolyi will continue to be a major presence on the U.S. women's gymnastics scene for the foreseeable future.

CHAPTER
5

Olga Korbut

The 1972 Olympics at Munich, Germany, are most memorable for two things, one terrible, the other beautiful.

The terrible event was the killing of eleven Israeli athletes in a terrorist attack.

The beautiful event was the appearance of Russian gymnast Olga Korbut.

Olga almost didn't make the Russian team. When one of the other gymnasts was injured, she got a last-minute call. As she marched out with her teammates, she looked completely out of place. Four feet eleven inches tall and weighing 85 pounds, Olga looked like some kid who had wandered in by mistake. With her blond pigtails bound up in yarn she looked about twelve years old. Actually she was seventeen.

There was another difference between Olga and her teammates. Most Russian gymnasts had been taught to hide their emotions. Olga was different. She smiled and waved at the crowd.

When Olga performed well her personality came through with a big smile. And when she made a mistake, she reacted to that as well. She had a chance to win a medal in the all-around competition. Then she committed a series of obvious errors during her uneven bars routine. She knew that she had lost her chance for a medal. When she went back to her chair she began to sob. Everyone in the arena, everyone watching television all over the world saw it. A spectator ran over and handed her a bouquet of flowers, but that seemed only to make things worse.

This genuine show of emotion captured everyone's heart. Americans had come to think of Russian athletes as emotionless robots, but Olga changed that.

There was, of course, much more to Olga than emotion. The next day she came back and gave a performance on the balance beam that looked absolutely impossible. She was able to do things no woman had ever done before in competition, and she did them to near perfection.

Olga Korbut of the former USSR performs on the balance beam in the 1972 Olympics in Munich, Germany. She won the gold medal in the event. (UPI PHOTO/CORBIS-BETTMANN)

In the end Olga Korbut won the gold medal on the beam, another gold in the floor exercises, and a silver on the uneven bars. And, of course, she had helped the Russians capture the team gold. She became the "Munchkin of Munich" and the "Darling of the Olympics."

Even though the United States and the then Soviet Union were still locked in the Cold War, the little Russian girl with the big smile was invited to the White House. She also met the Queen of England. But she liked Disneyland best of all.

Olga Korbut became so famous that thousands of fan letters addressed simply "Olga—Moscow" were delivered right to her. She had gone from an unknown last-minute replacement to the most famous woman gymnast in the world.

Olga is credited with starting the gymnastics craze in America. Before her appearance at the Olympics there were only 15,000 practicing gymnasts in America. Ten years later there were 150,000.

Perhaps it is not entirely fair to give all of the credit to Olga. A young American named Cathy Rigby won a bronze medal at the World Championships. She became the first American ever to win any sort of a medal in this high a level of competition. Cathy also performed at the 1972 games. While her performance wasn't at the same level as the Eastern European athletes', it was still respectable. People began to get the idea that you didn't have to be a Russian to be a good gymnast. In later years Cathy went on to become a gymnastics commentator and one of the chief promoters of women's gymnastics in America. She also appeared on Broadway as Peter Pan. She did not get great praise as an actress, but her flying scenes looked very natural.

Four years after her triumph in Munich, Olga Korbut returned to the 1976 Olympics in Montreal as captain of the then Soviet team. Her team won the gold medal in gymnastics, and Olga took a silver in the balance beam. But the Montreal Olympics were dominated by the astonishing Nadia Comaneci of Romania.

Olga retired from active gymnastics the following year and married Russian folk-rock singer Leonid Bartkevich. She worked for a while as a gymnastics coach. In 1986 she was living and working in the city of Minsk when disaster struck the Chernobyl nuclear reactor just a little over one hundred miles from where she lived. Since then she has devoted a great deal of her time and energy to raising money to help the victims of that disaster. Olga herself may be one of the victims. She now suffers from a thyroid condition that she attributes to radiation released in the accident.

Life has not been easy for many former Soviet athletes. At one time they were treated as national heroes and their future seemed assured. But the Soviet Union itself was crumbling by the late 1980s. In 1991 Olga and her husband moved to America where they joined their son who was already living here. They now live in Atlanta, where Olga eventually hopes to open her own gym. She has improved her English by watching American movies on television. She admits that one of the things she likes best is staying up late and watching television. And while she will not say that she misses her homeland she does say that at home she cooks a lot of Russian food, "Because that is the most delicious."

But she's happy. "I just have a chance to be a normal person."

Olga has absolutely no regrets about the years she spent in gymnastics. "Sometimes I say 'Enough . . . all my life I've done gymnastics. Let's do something else.' But I was born in gymnastics, and it is in my heart."

CHAPTER
6

Nadia Comaneci

It is safe to predict that there will never be another Nadia Comaneci.

After the 1972 Olympics it seemed impossible that any gymnast could become more famous than Olga Korbut. Then came Montreal 1976 and Nadia.

On the first day of the Olympics Nadia finished a spectacular routine in the uneven bars compulsory event. A few seconds passed and the scoreboard flashed 1.0. Bela Karolyi was furious. "Where is Nadia's score?" he bellowed. What Karolyi and the spectators didn't know was that the scoreboard could not register a 10. No one ever anticipated an athlete scoring higher than a

9.9. After all, a score of 10 would represent a *perfect* performance!

Then the announcement came over the public address system. "Ladies and gentlemen, for the very first time in Olympic history, Nadia Comaneci has received the score of a perfect ten!"

And it didn't end there. By the end of the competition Nadia had received seven perfect scores. That won her the gold in the all-around competition, a gold on the beam, another gold on the uneven bars, a bronze for floor exercises, and a silver for being a member of the second-place Romanian team.

That record has never been equaled. It has never even been approached.

Bela Karolyi had picked Nadia out as a future champion when she was only six. She wasn't his best student at first, but she worked harder than anyone else and there was no routine that she was afraid to try. By the time she was eight years old Nadia was the Romanian junior champion. At age eleven she was the best gymnast in the country. At thirteen she was European champion. So when she went into the Olympics at age fourteen she was not entirely unknown, but no one expected to see what they saw.

Nadia could do things in gymnastics that no

Nadia Comaneci strikes a perfect pose in her gold medal–winning balance beam routine at the 1976 Olympics in Montreal. (AP PHOTO/SUZANNE VLAMIS)

woman had ever attempted: double twists, double backward somersaults. She could perform some moves better than the people who had invented them. And she did all her moves consistently and with great style. Hers was an almost superhuman performance.

Olga had been all smiles and tears, her emotions right on the surface. And she gave great, if sometimes confusing, interviews. Nadia was the opposite. She rarely smiled and never cried. She didn't even say much. The world was fascinated by this tiny superstar gymnast but she didn't seem to care.

Bits and pieces of information came out. She had a collection of over one hundred dolls, all dressed in national costumes. She kept them lined up on a bench, for good luck, she said. It was one of the very few things about Nadia that made her sound like a typical fourteen-year-old.

But Nadia's carefully controlled life was about to be turned upside down. Shortly after the Montreal Olympics, the government took control of the Romanian women's gymnastics team.

Unfortunately, the Romanian government didn't know anything about running a gymnastics team. Without Karolyi to direct them, many of the girls, including Nadia, had their training routines disrupted. Many got completely out of shape. Nadia began losing meets and she began gaining weight. Unlike a lot of gymnasts who say they don't like sweets, Nadia loved them. She had athletes from other countries smuggle chocolate to her during competitions. As a result she gained over forty pounds.

She went on crash diets and took drugs to lose

weight. She lost her world title and at the age of sixteen she thought her career was over and began talking about retiring from gymnastics. There were all sorts of rumors about her physical and mental health.

She was miserable. She was a mess. In 1978 Nadia went back to Karolyi and begged him to train her again. Karolyi agreed and immediately put her on a brutal schedule of diet and exercise. In a few weeks she lost thirty-five pounds. Though she certainly wasn't in top shape for the World Championships she still managed to win on the balance beam.

When Nadia appeared at the 1980 Olympics in Moscow she was back in shape. At nineteen she was no longer one of Karolyi's elves. She was three and a half inches taller and twenty-one pounds heavier than she had been at Montreal. But she was still Nadia. She took the gold medal for the balance beam and floor exercise. Observers thought she should have taken the gold for the uneven bars as well. But she came in second to a Soviet gymnast in what some considered an unfair and openly political decision.

Nadia was a hero in Romania. And she was as closely guarded as any other national treasure. After Karolyi defected in 1981, she was closely watched by the Romanian secret police. She had planned to compete in the 1984 Olympics in Los Angeles. Then, just six weeks before the games, she announced that she had changed her mind and retired from gymnastics.

After that the outside world heard very little about her. She accepted a government coaching job. She was invited to the 1988 Olympics in Korea as an honored guest, but her government wouldn't allow her to attend. Nadia was so isolated that she was genuinely unaware of how famous she still was throughout the rest of the world. She doesn't say much about this time in her life.

In 1989 Nadia decided that she could no longer stand life in Romania. She escaped from the country with the help of a Romanian named Constantin Panait, who had settled in America. The escape was dramatic, like something out of a spy film. Nadia walked for hours in the dark, past armed guards and barbed wire fences until she finally found an opening in the fence at the Hungarian border. She then flew to the United States. It was November 28, 1989.

Nadia's troubles were far from over. Once she arrived in the U.S. Panait held her a virtual prisoner. When she tried to leave he would threat-en to have her deported. Since Nadia didn't know much English and had led an isolated life, she believed he could do this. Panait wanted Nadia to perform again and make endorsements, while he kept all the money.

As word of Nadia's situation got around some of her friends came to her aid. They helped her to leave Panait. Now Nadia Comaneci was finally truly free, for the first time in her life.

One of those who helped Nadia was the American gold medal–winning gymnast Bart Conner. They had met years earlier when she was fourteen and he was eighteen. Now they began an exhibition tour together. There was no public announcement but everyone in the gymnastics world knew their relationship was more than a professional one. It wasn't until 1994, on Nadia's thirty-third birthday, that Bart finally proposed to her. But Nadia believes in tradition. She had to have her father's permission to marry.

The Ceausescu regime had fallen, so the couple returned to Romania to ask Nadia's father Gheorghe, a car mechanic, for permission to marry. He agreed.

Nadia and Bart were finally married in April 1996. Together, they run a gymnastics academy in Norman, Oklahoma. Nadia has done endorsements for several major American companies. She was a gymnastics commentator for French and Romanian television at the Atlanta games.

The long and often unhappy story of the world's greatest woman gymnast seems to finally have a happy ending.

CHAPTER
7

Mary Lou Retton

When Mary Lou Retton was four years old she was inspired by watching Olga Korbut on television. But her real idol was Nadia. Like hundreds of thousands of other girls throughout the world, she wanted to be just like her.

Like Nadia, Mary Lou has become a champion. But in many respects she is very different from the silent and often lonely Romanian gymnast. Mary Lou is outgoing and enthusiastic—almost overwhelmingly so.

Mary Lou has always seemed tireless. When she was a child she was so spirited that her mother, Lois, put her in dancing school just so she could burn off some of her excess energy. But Mary Lou

Mary Lou Retton shows off her signature smile and her gold medal from the all-around competition at the 1984 Olympic games in Los Angeles. (UPI/CORBIS-BETTMANN)

was more of an athlete than a dancer. The Rettons were an athletic family. Father, Ron, had been a college basketball player at West Virginia University and a minor league baseball player. Mary Lou's three older brothers played basketball, baseball, and football. Her older sister was an accomplished gymnast.

After watching Nadia score all those perfect tens at the 1976 Olympics Mary Lou decided that gymnastics was going to be her life. She was a fast learner and by the age of twelve she was the best gymnast in her home state of West Virginia. But she knew she could only go so far in West Virginia. Mary Lou was dreaming of the Olympics and believed there was only one person who could help her fulfill that dream—Bela Karolyi.

Karolyi had seen Mary Lou perform and agreed to coach her. That meant she would have to move to Houston, where he had recently opened his gym. It was a tough decision, but it was what Mary Lou wanted and her family agreed to go along. So at age fourteen, Mary Lou moved to Houston.

She was completely focused on the Olympics, which were just a year away. She dropped out of high school and wouldn't graduate until years later. She spent all her time training or competing. She was so tired at the end of every day that she would just drop. She even slept right through a tornado that knocked a tree down on the house where she was staying.

At four foot nine and 100 pounds Mary Lou wasn't one of Karolyi's tiny little elves. She was built more like a miniature fullback. Karolyi called her "booboolina," which means fat. She got her weight down a bit, but throughout her career she was always known as a powerful, fearless gymnast rather than an artistic or graceful one. She also had a strong personality and was confident enough to handle her coach's famous pressure to excel.

Mary Lou got a chance to show what she had learned from Karolyi when Diane Durham, one of America's top gymnasts had to pull out of the 1983 McDonald's American Cup competition in Madison Square Garden. Mary Lou was called in as a replacement. By the time the competition was over she had won the vault and floor events, tied for first on the uneven bars, and won the all-around championship. She was no longer unknown.

After a spectacular showing in an international meet in Japan, Mary Lou was regarded as America's top female gymnast. She could do tricks that no other gymnast would even attempt. No American woman had ever won an Olympic gold medal in gymnastics, but Mary Lou was ready for the 1984 games.

Then, just six weeks before the opening ceremonies, she felt terrible pains in her knee. Within a short time she could hardly walk.

Mary Lou remembers this as the worst moment in her career. "My knee had been bothering me that whole year," she recalled, "but I didn't think much about it. But finally the knee had enough.

The cartilage had broken off and the joint was locked up. They took me to the emergency room, and the doctor nonchalantly said he was going to do surgery.

"I've always been a positive person, and I tried to remain positive. But the doctors were telling me there was no way I would go to the Olympics. I said, 'I've made it this far—no one's going to keep me from trying.'"

She had the surgery, and did the three months' worth of rehabilitation work in three weeks.

The 1984 games were held in Los Angeles and were boycotted by the then Soviet Union. Some of the best women gymnasts in the world were absent from competition. But Mary Lou faced real challenges nonetheless. The most formidable was Ecaterina Szabo of Romania. She, too, had trained with Karolyi, right before he left Romania.

The most dramatic competition came in the all-around, where Retton won by the narrowest of margins after scoring perfect 10s in the floor and vault events. The American crowd went absolutely crazy.

She also won the bronze in the individual floor exercise and uneven bars, silver for the vault, and a silver in the team competition. This was her Olympics.

In typically American fashion Mary Lou was

able to profit from her fame and success. She was the first female ever to appear on a Wheaties box. She had her own line of clothing and gave endorsements for McDonalds and half a dozen other major companies. It seemed that she was always on television, either in a commercial or giving an interview or as a sports commentator. She traveled the country giving motivational speeches, who better? At age sixteen she was a millionaire—a millionaire who still had to have her parents co-sign her contracts.

Mary Lou has handled her fame and fortune very well. She retired from competitive gymnastics in 1986. After getting her high school diploma she went to the University of Texas. There she met Shannon Kelley, the quarterback of the football team. They were married in 1990.

While she no longer seems to be on the TV screen twenty-four hours a day, she is hardly forgotten, and was a commentator at the Atlanta games.

Life has been very good to Mary Lou Retton. She has only one complaint: her weight. "If I didn't watch what I eat," she said, "I'd weigh three hundred pounds."

CHAPTER
8

The Events

Modern gymnastics began as a form of exercise, primarily for soldiers. Gymnastics for men was part of the second modern Olympic games in 1900. Women's gymnastics weren't part of the Olympics until 1928, and then only as a team event. Women did not compete in individual events until the Helsinki games in 1952. During the first half of the twentieth century the sport was considered too difficult and dangerous for most women.

Men's and women's gymnastics are still very different. Men compete in six skills: the vault, the high bar, floor exercise, the parallel bars, the pommel horse, and the rings. Women compete in four events: the vault, the uneven bars, floor exercise, and the balance beam. Although three of the events are the same for both men and women, the skills exhibited are still very different. Men's gymnastics rely mainly on power and strength. Women's gymnastics require strength as well, but they also incorporate grace and style.

The Vault
This event looks simple, but it isn't. The athlete sprints down the runway. At the end of the runway is a springboard. She launches herself off the springboard head first toward a piece of padded apparatus called the horse. For women the horse is 47 inches tall. The gymnast uses her hands to push off the horse, and lands in a standing position on the other side.

Sounds easy, but in vaulting over the horse the gymnast will also perform a series of twists and flips in the air and then hit the mat without taking a step. That's known as sticking the dismount.

This was the event that made a hero out of the injured Kerri Strug.

Floor Exercise
The gymnast performs a series of handsprings, somersaults, and other moves within a padded

area that measures twelve meters—a little over forty feet square. The exercise takes just over a minute.

Women perform the floor exercise to music, and the judges traditionally look for grace, balance, and emotional expression. But the women's performances have become increasingly athletic. "If they wanted to see dancing," observed Mary Lou Retton tartly, "they'd go to the ballet."

The Balance Beam

The gymnastics equivalent of tightrope walking, this event is performed only by women. The beam is sixteen feet long, four feet off the ground and four inches wide. Most gymnasts consider the beam the most difficult of all the events.

On this narrow strip of wood the gymnast must do somersaults, splits, handsprings, walkovers, cartwheels, back flips, and backward rolls using the entire length of the beam. Usually the gymnast will cover the entire length of the beam at least six times in a routine that lasts from seventy to ninety seconds.

Mounts and dismounts are also important and there are dozens of ways to perform these maneuvers as well.

The Uneven Bars

The most recent addition to gymnastics, the uneven bars were first demonstrated at the 1936 Olympics. They became part of the competition in 1952.

Women used to practice on the same sort of parallel bars or single bars that are used by the men. At some point, no one seems quite sure when, the arrangement of the bars was changed making one higher and one lower. This allowed women gymnasts to create routines that were based on grace and flexibility, not just strength.

The higher of the bars is 7.5 feet above the ground. The lower is 5 feet high. During a routine that lasts about thirty seconds the gymnast will do a variety of twists, somersaults, pirouettes, and changes of direction, using first one bar and then the other. She is allowed no more than five moves in a row on one bar.

Nadia Comaneci scored the first perfect 10 in Olympic history on the uneven bars.

Unlike a race, where there is a clear winner, gymnastics is scored by a panel of judges. Gymnastics scores tend to be subjective, controversial, and sometimes blatantly political.

Up through the 1996 games half of a gymnast's score came from the compulsories, or required exercises. These are skills that must be performed in a specific sequence. But from now on, the compulsories will no longer be a part of the Olympics or the World Championships.

In future Olympics, a gymnast's score will be based entirely on the optionals. Here the gymnast can, within certain well-defined limits, perform any movement she likes.

The events are judged by a panel of four to six judges, most of whom are former top gymnasts themselves. They give a score of up to 10 points for each performance. The highest and lowest scores of the panel are eliminated and the remaining scores are averaged to calculate the score for that routine. In Olympic or other world class gymnastics the competitors usually perform at such a high level that winners are determined by tenths of a point. A tiny mistake can mean the difference between a gold medal and no medal at all.

In the Olympics, the judges are chosen from different countries. Judges from one country may tend to award higher scores to the athletes from their home country and lower scores to the athletes who are competing against them. Perhaps that's not fair, but it is all too human. That is why the highest and lowest scores awarded by a panel of judges are thrown out.

But sometimes it seems that politics can overwhelm the sport. Nadia recalls that one of her worst moments in gymnastics came in the Moscow Olympics of 1980. She had to wait 28 minutes before the officials would post her score on the uneven bars. The reason was that there was a Russian girl competing, and the Russian officials wanted her to win. They wanted to see what score the Russian would get in a different event before they would give Nadia a score. As a result Nadia got only the silver medal in the all-around instead of the gold medal, which most observers believe she deserved.

From its introduction in the early years of the twentieth century, women's Olympic gymnastics has moved from an obscure event—one most women considered too unladylike to engage in— to what may be the most widely watched single sporting event in the entire world.

Highly controversial and highly political, it has made international celebrities and instant millionaires out of some of its stars. And it has very nearly ruined the lives of some others. But throughout the world it has sent millions of girls tumbling, swinging, and vaulting like their young heroes.

Despite its critics and its problems, women's gymnastics has become, and remains, one of the most beautiful, breathtaking, and inspiring of athletic events.

About the Authors

Daniel Cohen is the author of 150 books for children and adults. His recent titles include *Ghosts of the Deep*, *The Ghost of Elvis and Other Celebrity Spirits* and *Gus the Bear, the Flying Cat and the Lovesick Moose*.

Susan Cohen has written mystery and Gothic novels and has collaborated with her husband on a number of nonfiction books for young readers, including *Going for the Gold: Medal Hopefuls for Winter '92*.

The Cohens live in Cape May, New Jersey.